Mr. Daw Thought

by Frederick Prugh
illustrated by Nicole Rutten

Core Decodable 100

McGraw Hill Education

Bothell, WA • Chicago, IL • Columbus, OH • New York, NY

MHEonline.com

Send all inquiries to:
McGraw-Hill Education
8787 Orion Place
Columbus, OH 43240

ISBN: 978-0-02-136206-6
MHID: 0-02-136206-8

Printed in Canada.

9 10 11 12 KOD 24

Mr. Daw was so tired. He brought heavy loads of cheese into his shop all day.

Mr. Daw could not rest. He was going into a concert hall. His daughter had bought tickets.

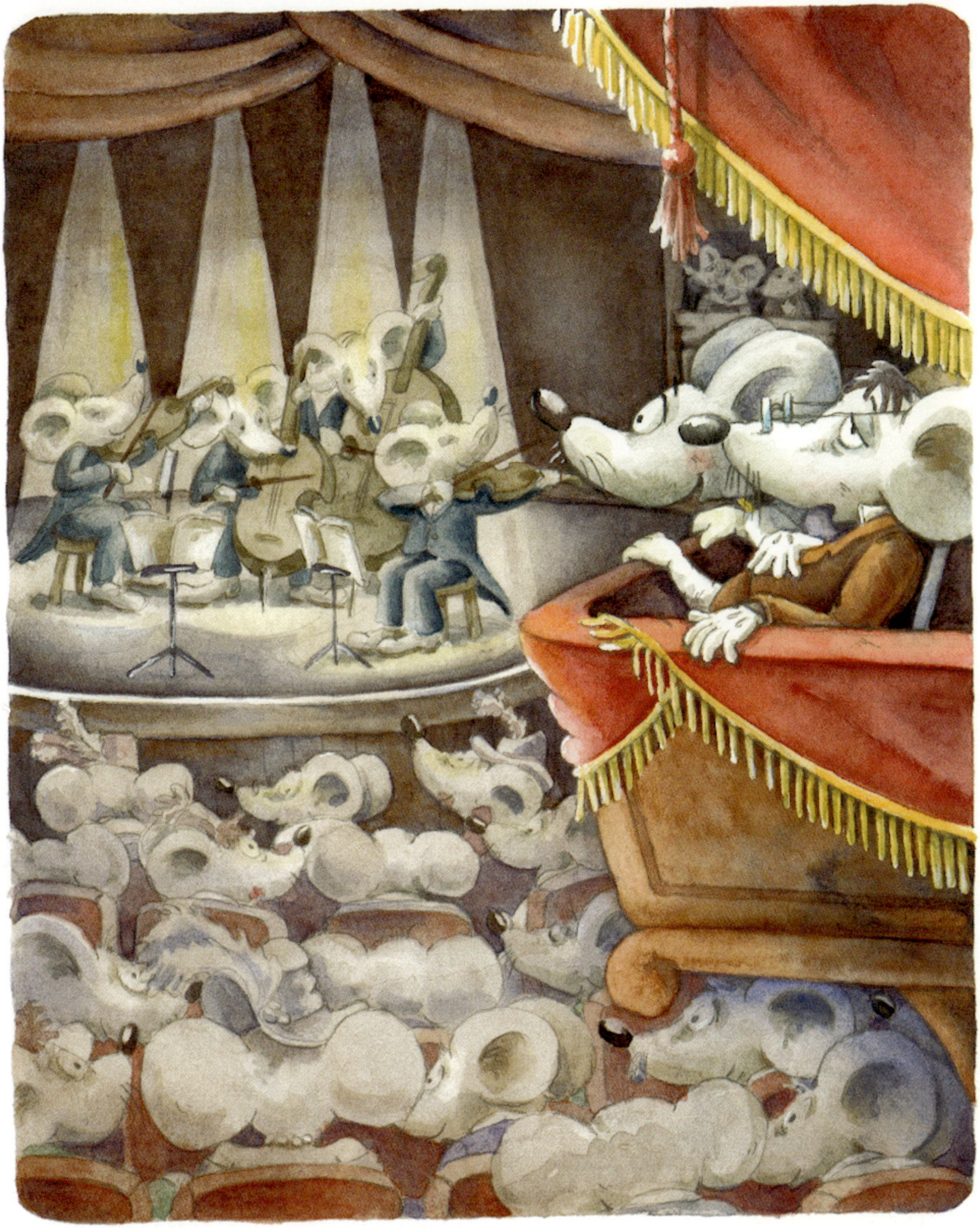

Mr. Daw liked music, but he was tired. He fought to stay awake as he sat in his seat.

Mr. Daw started to doze. His daughter sneezed into a cloth. He awoke.

"Don't get caught sleeping!" he thought.

Mr. Daw started to tap his foot. "Tapping ought to keep me awake," he thought.

The concert ended with applause.

"I am clapping for the music," he thought. "And because I stayed awake!"